The Pet Quiz

By Sally Cowan

"Get set, pets!" said Rib.

"It is The Pet Quiz!"

Pets get it at the vet.

It is **not** fun!

But it can fix pets up ...

A yak is too big for it!
But pets can get
to the vet in it ...

It can wag.
It can yap.
It can nap in the sun ...

CHECKING FOR MEANING

1. Who answered the first question? *(Literal)*

2. What was the yak too big for? *(Literal)*

3. How might Mits and Kit have felt when Pip and Bun won the quiz? *(Inferential)*

EXTENDING VOCABULARY

quiz	What are other words you know that rhyme with *quiz*? What do each of these words mean?
wag	What does it mean if a dog *wags* its tail? Why do dogs do this? What new words can you make if you take away the *w* and put another letter at the start?
win	How many sounds are in the word *win*? What are they? What is the small word at the end of *win*? Can you put a different letter at the start to make a new word?

MOVING BEYOND THE TEXT

1. What are other competitions that pets can go in?

2. If you could enter your pet in a competition, what pet would it be and what would you teach it to do?

3. Why is it important to take your pet to the vet?

4. How do you take your pet to the vet?

SPEED SOUNDS

Xx	Yy	Zz		
Kk	Ll	Vv	Qq	Ww
Dd	Jj	Oo	Gg	Uu
Cc	Bb	Rr	Ee	Ff	Hh	Nn
Mm	Ss	Aa	Pp	Ii	Tt

PRACTICE WORDS

Quiz

fix

yap

box

Yes

yak